SECRETS OF ANCIENT CIVILIZATIONS

THE LOST GOLDEN CITY OF LUXOR

by José Cruz

CAPSTONE PRESS
a capstone imprint

Published by Capstone Press, an imprint of Capstone
1710 Roe Crest Drive, North Mankato, Minnesota 56003
capstonepub.com

Copyright © 2025 by Capstone. All rights reserved. No part of this publication may be reproduced in whole or in part, or stored in a retrieval system, or transmitted in any form or by any means, electronic, mechanical, photocopying, recording, or otherwise, without written permission of the publisher.

Library of Congress Cataloging-in-Publication Data
is available on the Library of Congress website.
ISBN: 9781669087724 (hardcover)
ISBN: 9781669087885 (paperback)
ISBN: 9781669087687 (ebook PDF)

Summary: A royal city, long abandoned, was discovered by archaeologists in Egypt. Their findings changed what we thought we knew about the age of pharaohs, mummies, and pyramids! Discover the secrets of the Lost Golden City of Luxor.

Editorial Credits
Editor: Mari Bolte; Designer: Bobbie Nuytten; Media Researcher: Svetlana Zhurkin; Production Specialist: Whitney Schaefer

Image Credits
Alamy: dpa/Fadel Dawood, 25, 27; Getty Images: Mahmoud Khaled, cover, 5, 9, 10, 21, 23, 24, 29, 30, Photos, 12; The Metropolitan Museum of Art: Purchase, Edward S. Harkness Gift, 1926, 11, 17, Rogers Fund, 1915, 15, Rogers Fund, 1956, 20; Newscom: SIPA/Chine Nouvelle, 13; Shutterstock: Alejo Bernal (hieroglyphs), cover and throughout, art of line, 22, Bist, 8, Cholpan, 16, DongIpix (light rays), cover and throughout, hemro, 7, Massimo Todaro, 26, Peter Hermes Furian, 6, Sergey-73, 19

Any additional websites and resources referenced in this book are not maintained, authorized, or sponsored by Capstone. All product and company names are trademarks™ or registered® trademarks of their respective holders.

TABLE OF CONTENTS

INTRODUCTION
City in the Sand 4

CHAPTER 1
A Brief History of Ancient Egypt 6

CHAPTER 2
A Hidden Surprise 10

CHAPTER 3
The Dazzling Aten 14

CHAPTER 4
Digging Up Clues 20

CONCLUSION
The Golden City 28

City Timeline 30
Glossary 31
Learn More 32
Index 32
About the Author 32

Words in **bold** are in the glossary.

Introduction

CITY IN THE SAND

Deep within the blazing sands of Egypt, an amazing discovery has been made.

Looming walls tower over a tireless team of **archaeologists**. Another wall twists around the others like a coiled snake. Workers haul away **artifacts** such as buried treasure. Although the city is thousands of years old, it seems trapped in time.

What is this incredible place? It is the lost golden city of Luxor. This 3,400-year-old **metropolis** was uncovered by modern science. Historians say it is the second-most important discovery since the tomb of Tutankhamen, the famous boy **pharaoh**.

With every grain of sand that gets removed, it is clear that history is still not settled. There is always plenty that could change the way historians understand ancient Egypt.

After two months of digging, scientists uncovered several ancient neighborhoods.

Chapter 1

A BRIEF HISTORY OF ANCIENT EGYPT

The period known as ancient Egypt began around 3100 BCE. It was during this time that Egypt became unified as a country. It was ruled by Narmer, also known as Menes. His success and power was aided by the Nile River.

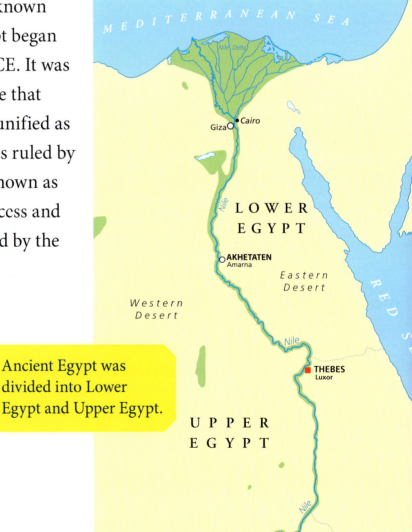

Ancient Egypt was divided into Lower Egypt and Upper Egypt.

The area surrounding the river is known as the Nile River Valley. It was extremely **fertile**. This made it perfect for farming. Egyptians were able to produce more crops than other countries. Having enough food to go around allowed the people to focus their attention on other areas. Egypt soon became known for its advances in construction and mathematics. Egyptians wrote their histories and recorded myths and legends. Their military was well-equipped and organized.

Painting, sculptures, and hieroglyphs tell historians about everyday life in ancient Egypt.

The Fall of an Empire

Throughout the years, ancient Egypt warred. Sometimes it won. But it was also conquered. After the rise of the Roman Empire, the native religion and language of ancient Egypt began to decline. The fall of the Roman Empire and more fighting brought an end to ancient Egypt around 395 CE.

The ancient Egyptians may be gone, but their monuments, like Karnak Temple, still remain.

The ancient Egyptians lived on through the things they left behind. Pieces of history, such as pyramids and **hieroglyphic** art, are physical proof of their existence. Mummified remains have given researchers a glimpse of everyday life. In some cases, whole parts of cities have been uncovered. The lost golden city of Luxor became the latest of these when it was discovered in 2020.

What was the purpose of this city? Why was it abandoned? And, perhaps most importantly, what happened to it? Like detectives solving a mystery, a team of archaeologists and other experts are working to discover these answers.

Ancient people used stone and mud bricks to build their homes.

Chapter 2

A HIDDEN SURPRISE

Zahi Hawass was the former Egyptian minister of **antiquities**. In September 2020, he set out on a mission. His team wanted to find the **mortuary** temple of Tutankhamen. This building would have held the gifts and offerings that were left for the pharaoh upon his burial.

The team focused on an area near the Egyptian city of Luxor. Other mortuary temples had been discovered here before. But instead of small structures, the team found walls—and lots of them.

Zahi Hawass has worked on digs across Egypt.

It became clear that the team had stumbled upon a **well-preserved** city. For years, it had been buried under the sand. The walls were made of mudbrick. They were marked with the stamp of Amenhotep III. This stamp allowed scientists to estimate how old the city was. It also told them who the pharaoh was when it was built. Official confirmation of the discovery was made on April 8, 2021.

Cartouches contained hieroglyphs of a pharaoh's name, such as Amenhotep III, inside an oval.

A Stunning Success

Another mud seal revealed the city's name. It was called "the dazzling Aten." Aten was the Egyptian sun god. Historians already knew that the city of Aten existed. Other records had mentioned it. But all attempts to pinpoint its location had failed, including a French expedition in 1934.

The god Aten was shown as a disc casting long rays. Each ray ended in a hand.

In 2023, Hawass's team announced that they had uncovered about half a square mile (1.3 square kilometers) of the city's southern side. They said there was much more left to find to the north and east. The artifacts they already found help experts gain a clearer understanding of what life in ancient Egypt was like. Like pieces of a jigsaw puzzle, each discovery fit together to show how "the dazzling Aten" came to be.

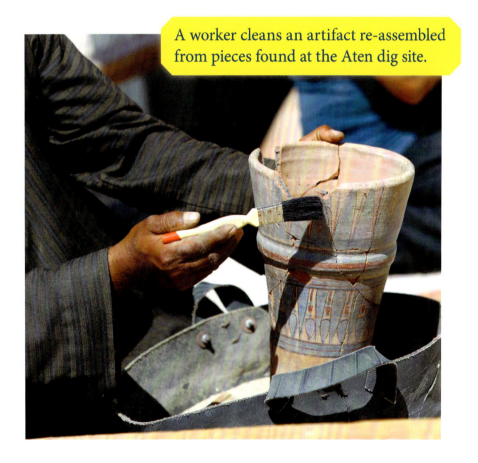

A worker cleans an artifact re-assembled from pieces found at the Aten dig site.

Chapter 3

THE DAZZLING ATEN

During the **reign** of Amenhotep III, Thebes was the country's capital. Today, we call it Luxor. Amenhotep III was the wealthiest pharaoh ever to rule ancient Egypt. Because he never went to war with other countries, he was able to gain large amounts of wealth. He used his extra money on special projects.

One of these projects was the construction of a new city. This sister city was built nearby. It was part of the pharaoh's palace complex and would be filled with building-lined streets inside towering walls. The construction occurred sometime between 1386 and 1353 BCE. Hawass called his find the "Golden City" of Luxor, since it was built during ancient Egypt's golden age.

Amenhotep III sits on his throne. His mother stands behind him.

The New Pharaoh

After Amenhotep III passed away, his son took control. Amenhotep IV wasn't ruler for long before he began making big changes. First, he ended worship of all the Egyptian gods except for Aten. Next, he changed his name from Amenhotep IV to Akhenaten. This translates to "devoted to Aten." Finally, the pharaoh moved the capital from Luxor to an entirely new city he named Akhetaten in 1336 BCE. Today, Akhetaten is called Amarna. Over his 17-year rule, the pharaoh upended the Egyptian way of life.

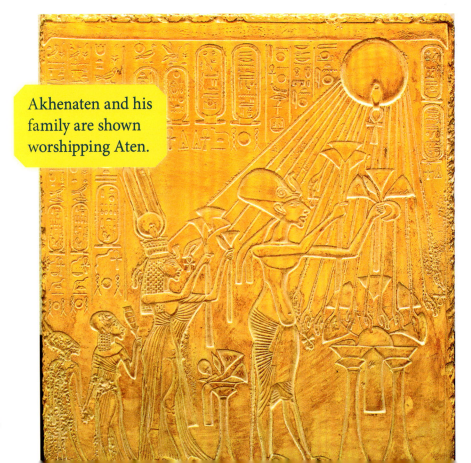

Akhenaten and his family are shown worshipping Aten.

The Gods Return

After Akhenaten's death, the next ruler was his son, Tutankhamen. Tutankhamen ordered the temples dedicated to other Egyptian gods to be reopened. The god Aten was abandoned in favor of the new sun god, Amun. Amun (later called Amun-Ra) would become much more popular than Aten. Amun, the "king of the gods," was even worshipped outside of Egypt in other countries.

A statue of Amun made of gold can be seen at the Met Museum in New York City.

Why did the pharaoh make all these sudden changes? Historians still aren't sure. But his decisions were not liked by many of his subjects. They felt that Akhenaten had changed their way of life too quickly. When Akhenaten passed away, Tutankhamen purposefully erased large parts of his father's work.

Akhenaten and his temple were not rediscovered until the early 1700s. People lived among the ruins of his city, but their origin went unknown for hundreds of years. But records were found and tombs were uncovered, giving historians clues to what was once there. If it wasn't for the pursuit of history, the pharaoh—and his legacy—might have been lost to the sands of time forever.

The ruins of Akhetaten contain houses, temples, cemeteries, and palaces.

Chapter 4

DIGGING UP CLUES

Historians already knew about Amenhotep III and his son, Akhenaten. They also knew about the city of Aten long before the discovery in 2020. But they knew there was even more to uncover. Archaeologists knew Aten was the main site of administration and labor during that time. A huge amount of information about its peoples' everyday lives was ready to be found.

The tomb of Amenhotep III was first discovered in 1799.

Life in the City

The lost golden city of Luxor appears to have been split into two sections. The industrial section was for shops and workplaces. The residential section was where people lived. A bakery was discovered in the industrial section. Inside was an oven and a place to prepare meals. They also found containers for storing food. One of these sealed pots contained dried meat. The outside of the pot listed the names of the people who made it.

FACT

Reports claim that at one point Aten was the largest settlement in all of ancient Egypt. It is the largest Egyptian city ever discovered.

A variety of pottery has been uncovered at the Aten site.

Strange Structures

A unique zigzag wall surrounds the city. It is up to 9 feet (2.7 meters) tall in some places. Historians have been interested in its purpose from the beginning. Walls like this were not a common sight in ancient Egypt. Experts believe that it might have been meant to act as security for the citizens. But its true purpose remains a mystery.

S-shaped walls curve along the entire city.

Hawass's team also discovered an underground cemetery. There were tunnels and staircases carved from rock. One of the strangest finds was the skeleton of a bull or cow inside its very own burial chamber. A human skeleton was also found. Its arms were extended and ropes were wrapped around its knees.

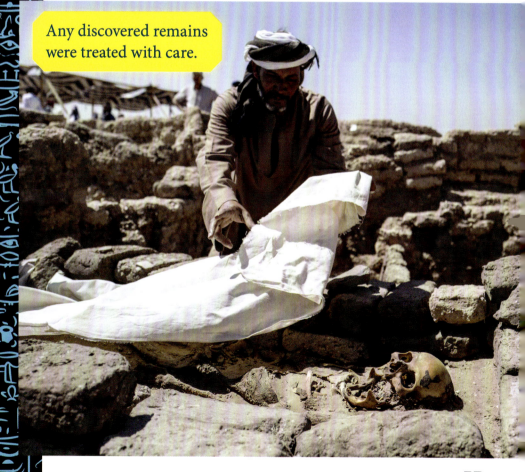

Any discovered remains were treated with care.

Life and Play

The objects found inside the city walls told experts about the people who lived there. Jewelry and glassware were found inside the **excavated** buildings. Craftspeople had time to create beautiful, rather than practical, pieces.

Jewelry and pottery are only some of the items found inside Aten's buried walls.

Thousands of small pieces help historians put together a larger picture of ancient life.

More discoveries included children's dolls and gaming pieces made from limestone. Staying out of war during Amenhotep III's reign meant more money and more time to play. People could pay others to make their food and build things for them.

Frozen in Time

Aten's level of preservation has been compared to Pompeii. Pompeii was an ancient city in Italy. A volcanic eruption preserved it. A lost city in the desert sands has given us the same kind of treasures from the past.

The city of Pompeii was abandoned nearly 2,000 years ago.

It can take a long time to restore artifacts into complete pieces.

Experts are still learning about Aten and the rule of Akhenaten. Was the city truly abandoned during the years when the capital was moved to Akhetaten? What happened between fathers and sons to force such drastic changes? Will more pieces of the city be uncovered in the future?

There are still pieces of the puzzle being discovered. Each new piece gives historians a more complete picture of what life was like at one of the richest times in ancient Egypt's history.

Conclusion

THE GOLDEN CITY

Archaeologists have only just begun to rediscover the lost golden city in Luxor. Though some questions have been answered, many more mysteries remain. Historians hope to find out why Akhenaten abandoned Amenhotep III's city. They want explanations for the human and animal burials. The zigzag wall must have a purpose. But what?

Historians expect to find never-before-seen tombs full of artifacts and treasures. Perhaps one of them will provide an answer to these puzzling questions.

Modern life is not so different from life in ancient Egypt. People played, cooked, and shopped. They created art. They lived in homes and cities. But the details of their lives have been lost to time. Scientists, archaeologists, historians, and other experts make discoveries that shed light on those lives. The dazzling Aten will shine again.

The discovery of the lost golden city was one of the most exciting moments of Zahi Hawass's career.

CITY TIMELINE

CIRCA 1386-1353 BCE: The city of Aten is built.

1336 BCE: Akhenaten abandons the city of Aten.

1934 AND 1935: French archaeologists attempt to discover Aten.

2020: Egyptian expedition begins to excavate Aten.

2021: Egyptian expedition confirms discovery.

GLOSSARY

antiquities (an-TIK-wuh-tees)—objects used in an earlier time

archaeologist (ar-kee-OL-uh-jist)—a scientist who studies how people lived in the past

artifact (AR-tuh-fakt)—an object used in the past that was made by people

excavated (EK-skuh-vay-ted)—dug out of the earth

fertile (FUHR-tuhl)—having many nutrients

hieroglyphic (hye-ruh-GLIF-ik)—having to do with an early form of writing that used picture symbols called hieroglyphs

metropolis (muh-TRAW-puh-luhs)—a large and densely populated city

mortuary (MOR-choo-air-ee)—a place used to store bodies

pharaoh (FAIR-oh)—an Egyptian king

reign (RAYN)—to rule

well-preserved (WELL-pri-ZURVD)—kept in good condition for a long period of time

LEARN MORE

Loh-Hagan, Virginia. *Ancient Egypt*. Ann Arbor, MI: Cherry Lake Publishing, 2021.

O'Neill, Sean. *50 Things You Didn't Know about Ancient Egypt*. South Egremont, MA: Red Chair Press, 2020.

Britannica Kids: Luxor
kids.britannica.com/students/article/Luxor/49461/media

National Geographic Kids: Ancient Egypt
kids.nationalgeographic.com/history/article/ancient-egypt

INDEX

Akhenaten, 16–19, 20, 27, 28, 30
Amenhotep III, 11, 14–16, 20, 25, 28
Amenhotep IV. *See* Akhenaten
Amun, 17
artifacts, 4, 13, 27, 28
Aten (god), 12, 16, 17

construction, 7, 14, 30

farming, 7
Hawass, Zahi, 10, 13, 14, 23, 29
hieroglyphs, 7, 9, 11

Menes. *See* Narmer
military, 7
mummies, 9

Narmer, 6
Nile River, 6, 7

pyramids, 9
Roman Empire, 8

tombs, 4, 18, 20, 28
Tutankhamen, 4, 10, 17, 18

walls, 4, 10, 11, 14, 22, 24, 28

ABOUT THE AUTHOR

José Cruz is an elementary school media specialist based in Southwest Florida. His journalism and short fiction have appeared in print and online, including best-of collections. His favorite topics deal with the dark, the strange, and the mysterious.